Anointing in My Hands

by

Jacqueline Gillon

Copyright 2010 by Jacqueline Gillon

Anointing in my Hands

ISBN: 978-0984324538

Published by: ***Parablist Publishing House, Inc.***

Email: <u>parablistpublishing@yahoo.com</u>

Web: parablistbooksonline.com

All rights reserved solely by the author. The author guarantees all contents are original and do not infringe upon the legal rights of any other person or work. No part of this book may be reproduced in any form without the permission of the author.

Author's photo by McKinley Wiley

Introduction

Anointing In My Hands is a dream alive after years of writing, reciting , pausing only to write again. It was sixth grade after the assassination of Dr. King, as I stood outside Chambers Elementary School in East Cleveland, Ohio. The empty streets echoed the profound pain that came with the violent departure of our leader. This impression left me only one choice: to script my sorrow. As a child growing up in the sixties, I felt the presence of God in my life over and over again, through joy or sadness; seeing the beauty of the world and benefitting from the blessing of family and community.

Now I am approached to poetically respond to life-changing events: marriages, the passing of family members and birthdays. Poems, for me, often come from the voice of God through worship and nature. Relationships through blood, bond, consciousness or community tickle the imagination.

May the anointing transform you in some way as well.

Table of Contents

Tribute to a King (7)

Amen Corner (8)

Blessed Peace (10)

Choose Life (12)

Church (14)

Daughter of the Wind (15)

Denied Access (17)

Engaging (18)

Eric's Gone Home (1)

Facebook Love (21)

Flaunting Fifty (22)

Giving Up Times (24)

Homework (27)

Hungry (29)

I Have Miracle Eyes (31)

In The Light (33)

It's Me Lord (35)

Little Things (36)

Mercy on Me (37)

Moving Through the Storm (39)

Love of a Lifetime (40)

Bridges (42)

God's Family Trust (45)

Letting Go (47)

Never Seen the Color Blue (48)

New Day (50)

Praise Him (51)

Reasons (52)

Reflection (53)

Surrender (55)

Sweet Spot (56)

The Rock and the Hard Place (57)

Tia Supreme (60)

The Joy (62)

We Are Not (64)

We Called Her Ms. Treadway (66)

Tribute to a King

A peaceful man was King,

who believed that freedom should ring

through mountain and valley

for black and for white,

let freedom ring,

let freedom sing for all.

King won the Nobel Prize,

but his example was greater in size.

We shall overcome, we shall overcome,

we shall overcome someday

But we shall overcome in King's non-violent way.

1968 age 11

Amen Corner

For Deborah and Pamelia

I come to you Lord

and you say yes

When I am stressed

and questioning

what to do

When my life seems out of control

you say yes

Come and rest with me

So many things I desire to do

How will they all get done?

How will I get through

this race I must run?

You say yes

Of course you can come

to this Amen Corner

I will bless

and give rest

in the Amen Corner.

Blessed Peace

The brush of the wind

against your cheek

is her kiss sweet

Strong soft voice

in your ear

is the sound of love

that dances in the trees

Each time you honor God

Is when she'll smile

Facing the darkness of life

was the courage of her resolve

The best way to miss her

is to give your heart to God

And her spirit will fill with joy

The rainbow appeared

Three times in the sky

She was blessed

With a son

Each one the apple of her eye

The memory of her kindness

Laughter and loyalty

And the way she loved shoes!

Will shield you from the emptiness

you'll sometimes feel.

Unimaginable pain has ceased.

The transforming gift of time

will increase

As her spirit settles in blessed peace.

Choose Life

In His divine mind

He liberated mankind

We have the choice to surrender to the

Magnificent or mundane

We crawl on our bellies

Fly through the air

Do we care

Embrace the magic

Make the money

Play the music

Catch the train

Take the time

To sip the sublime

Love the children

Make that deadline

We choose

Life meaning things

Shop 'til we drop

Fall on our knees

Forgive and not forget

We can choose to

Clear the clutter

Muster the energy

Never forget a kindness

We choose life

Play ball or not at all

Exercise our God-given gifts

We choose life –meaning things

Choose…

Church

The body of the letter is truth

The body of believers is the

God Mind

standing in a transforming time

Holy Spirit moves with

a weapon of peace

Faith finding space

in our cynical hideaways

Feet touching common ground

The scales balance.

Daughter of the Wind

I first remember sitting at her feet

as she tugged at rebellious hair

Telling me everything

without saying a word

except

"Be still"

I watch as she dresses

as she toils

as she lives

Daughter!

Bursting from Mother Earth

Inheriting the dignity and dazzle

Of days gone by

Mother!

Planting seeds of hard-fought courage

And secrets of femininity

It is so delightful watching as she

dances in the wind

To stop

and pick her child up

To stir a pot

To shed tears of joy and pain

And never giving it another thought

I am the jewel of her dreams

I am her measured thought

Her elbow grease

Her whispered prayers

and every good night she shared

I am my mother's legacy

I am the daughter

Of the wind

Denied Access

The innocent and the ignorant nestle in assigned conclaves

Never wondering why

If creature comforts do not escape

Not to bother, not to bother to

Unearth the truth or master manipulate.

The gates of hell are open.

How can you destroy the earth,

enjoy the unholy mirth

practicing privilege at the greedy man's knee

while conclaves are huddled losing breath and comfort

God-given longevity interrupted

By the oiling of the seas

Corruption of the air

Never imagining tomorrow is responsibility

Humanity belongs to all

Even if denied access…

Engaging

Unconditional ignites the flame of interlude

and realization …

God's children are made for love

It is His plan that it becomes an intimate proposition

In sacred agreement we come

Mystery unfolding lights the heart

and spills the glow of faith and trust

You are the mirror to my soul.

Soul mates contemplate the pod and promises.

Eric's Gone Home
For Julie

The children come proud and sad

As we with more time to have seen

Heroes and Heroines fall

Celebrate and mourn

The victory, the battle

As he is set free, set free

Slipping from a mother's grasp

As family, friends and strangers gasp

In a quickening glance we bare witness to

Sweet youth aged in grace and wisdom

brave and willing enough

to live daring and free

sailing away on a glory ride

tender mercy no longer concealed

as we melt pain with tears

he lived lovely and fierce as his words

no more pain merchants

dealing ignorance and fear

departing stories are pictures

bright as autumn leaves

bright and playful pictures

mothers, uncles, cousins

aunts, teachers and friends

teammates and best friends

cuddle and huddle

telling laughter and tears

lifting life long and short

neat and complete

legacy opening and closing the door.

Facebook Love

I want you to know

That you touch my soul

What better way for me

To say

I love you so.

I want you around

It's hard I know

To see the way

You got my attention now

Somehow you have found

A place in my heart

Right from the start

You touch my soul…

Flaunting Fifty
For Donna J.

This is not a diva act of rebellion

We are not selling inappropriate

can't accept it

Denial

This is the launching of wrapping happy around grace

It is the face of ageless under fire

Desire is skillfully dancing

No more blocking blessings

Believing we are less than we

are created to be

Faith is the key

Of wearing 50 like new money

time to play it very cool

Haven't done all the things

knowing your purpose brings

Humbly sophisticated Mother, Grandmother

Auntie and friend

Just shake this moment loose and free

Our chance to flaunt how

Maturity grows elegantly

We got it

working through it

Thankful

to God Almighty

Flaunting Fifty!!!!!!!!!!!!!!!!!!!!!!!!!!!

Giving Up Times

This is the part

When you fold your wings in

And tuck away your heart

And I get to figure out

what that tense grin means

This is the part when you go

Into that suitcase where

You left last life's dreams

To see if they are still

Alive

Folded up in a dusty paradise

Somewhere

This is the part when tears are salty

And nights are endless

And days are occupied occasions

Of distraction

This is the part when we're

Supposed to say goodbye

And I know this part so well

I repeat your lines from

Memory

Re-runs and waiting for

The sun to rise

Are my lines and so

Is goodbye

This is the part when we can save

Ourselves

If we could just remember that

First smile and the next

Hello

And how we danced

And the moon and

How the conversation grew

And giggles between kisses

And listen to what

Happy is

This is the way we can say HELLO…

Homework

I heard a song the other day

That asks us where is the place where

Shame and grace meet

I ask my beloved community

On this day

Where is the place where

We feel most unloved?

Can we start there

To repair the breach

The broken connection

That hidden reflection

That needs to come to view.

We know we hurt each other

We know we cause each other pain!

In the name of politics, money or fame

It doesn't matter

That is our shame!

It is time for grace to find us

Whether it is institutional righteousness

Or the need to say I can

Because I can

The wound is our psyche

That begs for healing

Let grace find it

And bind it

We can say goodbye to

Crushing competitiveness

We can say goodbye to

Depressing isolation

We can say goodbye

To privileged arrogant loneliness

Let grace find us…

Hungry

When you are not sure

Anything can inform your doubt

The compliments are nice yet fleeting,

And the criticisms can haunt you.

Silence can distract or destroy.

Turn to Him when you need to see

Your beauty or brilliance

And to open your heart to love

When you are not sure

If that guy loves you

Or if that lady is truly for you

When your child is not recognizable

When your body or heart aches

When the time comes to let go

He gives you the power to believe

And the strength in your times of need

When you are not sure

Open up wide

The Lord will feed your faith…

I Have Miracle Eyes

I have miracle eyes to see

light and energy growing

love inside me

I am planted tree

flower blossomed

I flow and glow

colors of gladness

Content because I am

Waking to another chance

To touch in communion

And renewal

It's really okay to be a tree

In one season

Buds love blossom

In another

Shedding leaves like tears

But in due season shaking with laughter free

My back arching finding a forgiving stance

One season a dance,

Another as fragile body clinging to the sky

Stark and naked as pain

In due season I see me again

I bend and stretch my branches to the sky

And smile.

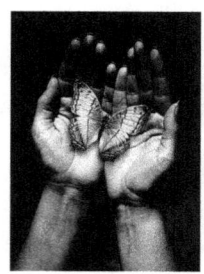

In The Light

We are journey renewed

We are traveling wise and wonderful

Spirit-filled and glowing

Facing darkness and lifting light

Gentle spirit all knowing

Gives us one tenth showing

At a time

Don't forget the mission traveler

No omission of lessons learned

Practice and teach

Inspire and preach

Drop the pretense

Times are intense

Wrap love around words

Take a journey

Flow through trouble

Flow history through darkness

Flow knowledge

Into the light

Take a journey

Sing sorrow soothing

Choose words building

Don't forget the lesson traveler

Surrender control

God's road map unfolds

Take a journey

It's Me Lord

Tall as the sky my dreams and I reach

for the fingertips of God

To touch and agree,

I begin trusting

Just reach and stretch

connect and respect

all that He has prepared us to be

No more fear to love or forgive

To learn and to live

The blessing is the ability to give

Stand in your greatness and climb to the sky

Never mind you might have to cry

Open your mind and try

Come closer to Him

Don't deny

Stand in your greatness

And reach to the sky

Little Things
For My Mother

New sky

Joining peaceful river

Shimmering from the encouragement

Of soft wind blows

Welcoming birds to breakfast

And appointed adventure

This is my morning bouquet.

Give the flowers now

While there is a sun and moon dance

To enjoy

Share a meal of listen and nod

A hug that holds a moment of

Comfort and strength.

Show your devotion now!

Life is now energy

God-gifted gratitude.

Mercy on Me

Had I not found you here

In the midst of the beginning and

Ending of time

I would have waited

Like a mother for her child

A farmer for the harvest

I would have waited

Until another time

Like this

For the newness of the revelation

For your attention

Though I am not good at this

I fluctuate between the flesh

And the spirit

Calling out your name

Pleasure I feel in my ear

My heart and soul peaceful

As prayers and scripture

Draw us near

Still it is my assignment

To wait until the ink dries

And the books are balanced

And we no longer

Fear the challenge.

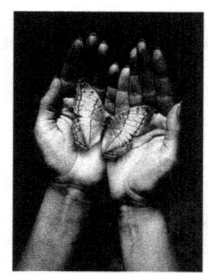

Moving Through the Storm

Been stormin' in my sky lately

But I'm gonna be alright...

Been cloudy in my life lately

Mercy is my cover

as the raindrops come.

Don't know when we'll see heaven

Wanna stay here awhile and

reflect the sunshine of His love

It's been storming in my sky lately

But I'm gonna be alright...

'Cause I know we'll see the sun

Praise God for the changes

We're all going to see the sun

While rain falls softly

The healing surely comes.

Love of a Lifetime
Wedding Poem #3

For
Eryka and Doug
Daria and Jeffrey

This is the place

Where time stands still

And we witness the light

Much brighter

As the dawn comes sooner

The night sets the stage

For the mystery of love

To unfold

This is the moment we recognize

The commitment

Love has finalized

We can rejoice

That our hearts

Have found a home

The hour has come

That our lives

Will write a new day

This is the way

We wrap love around children

Hope surrounding friends

These are the steps

Appointed by the King

This is the place our hearts

Will memorize

This is the love of a lifetime

Bridges

The early ones were made of rope

knotted and twisted together and reinforced

to be strong and durable

so that animal, man or cargo could be carried

across to reach its destination.

Then came

wood and bolts

concrete and steel girding

all designed to connect across

valleys and by-ways, rivers and lakes

Trusted not to fall

maybe to lean or creak

Cracks appear from use and age

demanding reinforcement

A span across to other places

that is the value

we gain from bridges

Some folks build bridges

A few repair them

But some of us are bridges

willing to be strong

to reach out in action or deed

bearing the weight of the issue

planning to fulfill the mission

connected by whatever

sturdy materials are available.

We lay down time and principle

To span across poverty, ignorance

Isolation or fear

Trusted not to fall

Maybe to lean or creak

From long use and age

We need reinforcement sometimes

But by design we're intended

To last for awhile

That is the price we pay

For being a bridge.

God's Family Trust

Forever flowing from his coffers are riches

He loans us brothers by blood or bond

The master's bank of talent and knowledge

His wisdom and joy unfolding in our brothers

Silver coins fall and perch as leaves on trees

And flower petals as sisters

Growing to create jewels of insight, sweet affection

And tender security

Earthly fathers stand as the keepers of God's golden gates

Of protection and counsel

A wealth of love flows through the arms of strong men

giving proper provision and wisdom

God has painted masterpieces of immeasurable

beauty and value

Mothers of dignity and unyielding determination are the

The stocks and bonds of his treasury

Deposited within their hearts is the power of the ages

Unto himself he swiftly gathers his loaned gifts

The essence of which is eternal

So that he may multiply and gratify His creation.

Letting Go

Tree stumps like brown bodies growing green vines

going nowhere

Do we care that our lives can be fertile ground

If it sounds like hope is alive, it is it is

Smiles that no longer show love

Eyes, hard with age and disappointment

hold fast to traditional trysts with

What we used to do blues

I love you, I love you but you are breaking my heart

We have to press forward, our children can't wait

Press forward to the high calling

Jesus was a non-conformist

Bringing the kind of love that old school didn't understand

Press forward with courage

Bring the wisdom of the past

But it won't last

If you don't bring it.

Never Seen the Color Blue

We don't always walk the same walk

Talk the same talk

Things that I am clueless about

Useless for you to try to convince me

That I should know, that I should see

You have to teach me.

By opening ourselves up to give and receive.

We all have some darkness

We walk in

There are things we just can't conceive

Caught up in being you and me

All I know is I found you

In my heart

But you don't know what that means

All that is known is the blindness of pain

And that's what you given me

again and again

I am stumbling

You are wounded.

Though my heart is open

Yours is not

You weren't ready for that lesson in school

Just maybe you've never seen the color blue.

New Day
For James

Honey flows through my mind

thoughts filling available moments

pondering your easiness

Just when I stop listening to love songs

Or writing poems that reflect spirit sublime

I find your eyes and a

Methodical mind taking time

to force gentle reflection

Of my story before you discovered me

splintered and off-key

jagged edges smoothed patiently

I cannot hide blues or my joyous rhythms

From you

Your laugh soothes with consideration

and the song is new again

Flowing honey sweet…

Praise Him

Praise Him through fire,

Praise Him through rain,

Praise Him when the sun shines,

Praise Him through the pain.

Healing' s going to happen....

Praise Him again!

Reasons

The reasons why not

Create the seasons

When we fly

All the things that

Come between us

Give us the wings

That set us free

The more you hold back

The more you need to give.

Reflection

I have been filled so many ways by your presence

Not that I was ever empty

Maybe hungry for a space of safety and imagination and

investigation

Of me and Spirit and Emotion

Responsibility and Truth

Roads that I needed to travel

You met me there

Your water is very deep

We share the benefit of mutual solitude

And the self-centeredness of it too

Here is where God can reach you

Alone in tears and research and prayer

Within an attitude of receivership

Here is where I found you

We released and screamed and teased and informed

Held sacred in thoughts, memories and ideas.

Unfettered by drink or smoke and little frolic

You Love and Think and contain Spirit raw and pure

Like the forest takes in the sun and the rain

And the earth seed

And the air sound.

On really good days we laugh to tears

From imitations you secretly do so well

I love you so much

You have released me from your arms and your kisses

And your deeply passionate ways

Now they make me more of what I am

Lovely and poetic

As you are

On a really good day.

Surrender

Back to the open arms of a God that really loves me

Been feeling kind of lonely and out-of tune

Folks can say, no, no not you but

Graciously He waits for me to say

Lord I really love and need you too

Got a lot of questions and not enough patience

Help me to yield to the One who will see me through

Believe me I'm grateful that You have kept me thus far

I want to serve and live in a different way now.

But Lord I don't know how.

Thought my life would have been different

at this turn in the bend

I can't pretend disappointment hasn't tried to be my friend.

My prayer is for strength

Strength to uncover the path He has laid out

And the woman He has called me to be

Faithful and trusting…

Sweet Spot

Found a piece of heaven in your eyes

The light of God in your smile

Standing in the need of your love now

Finding myself in this sweet spot

You ask me what motivates my heart

It's always the little things from the start

The way you pay attention

Your tenderness and patience

Finding myself in this love stance

Needing a second and a third chance

To settle into joy that's heaven-sent

Free to be myself

in all my complexity

Found acceptance just in time

God gives us the unlimited

And it's truly divine

Find me in this sweet spot that's right on time

Waiting patiently for my chance

To share some time in this sweet spot…

The Rock and the Hard Place

Here and there

Up and down

The kiss and the hug

Head and shoulder, baby 1,2, 3!

What happens in between

Getting here and leaving

Are the billable hours

What we do for Christ, the Village, our Karma

Is the whole ball of wax

The fact that we arrived here safely and we definitely have to leave

Puts a slight tilt on the real meaning of things.

How you looked

Or how much you had in your pocket is inconsequential

You know what I mean?

Did you love someone?

Did you love yourself?

Was the place warmer after you left?

Or will they be glad when you're gone

You got the ball

But did you pass it on so somebody else could hoop?

Or you think it's just your show?

What happens between the opening act and the closing curtain is the story

Not where you bought the costume!!

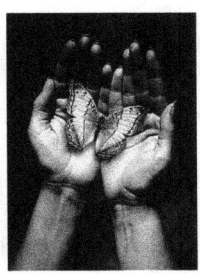

Tia Supreme

For Marvelous and Markietta

Brilliant eyes bright

Blaze a vision

Of order and insight

Babies come and are christened

A gift or two

A kiss and a pretty thing

All pretty things

In perfect order

Unique and sassy

Set aside for

One special way

Of living and giving

Her love is not tucked away

But on display in legacy

Not lost but fulfilled

In a jazzy way

An unselfish way

All the pretty things

Connected just so

A special touch

She leaves on the heart.

The Joy
Wedding Poem #4
For Heidi and Jonathan

Finding faith in the mystery of love

by trusting the sacred timing of God's will

Dream

awakening us this day

In the beauty of unity

Wrapped in a cover created

By the Almighty

Walking in the path of joy

We cherish each moment as a gift

Rejoicing as fresh blessings begin

Knowing that the path may narrow

The hour may darken

But the joy is evermore

Witness the miracle of patience

The sweet tenderness of adoration

As our family shares in the promises

And the wonders of the joy.

We Are Not

We are not the burdens of the day

Or the sickness and weakness

That might come our way

We are not wealth or fame

Power or shame

We are not money

We are not clothes or houses

Or all the things we like to do

We are not the business or the political review

We are life and breath

We are light and energy

We are not past or the future

We are now

Whole and accountable

Glowing and insurmountable

We are kisses and hugs

Gleam of eye and dream

We are already purchased

So we wear priceless on our sleeve

Bear witness with me

We are not the nightmare or the destruction

Or terror

These things may come our way

But we were not created that way

We are the hope

We are the faith

We are the ones

Who are saved…

We Called Her "Ms. Treadway"
For Mark

More than fifty years my mother's good friend

Gave me my beautiful name

Power of womanhood

Captured in her graceful gait

The strength of stand

A chuckle of wisdom

That working hand

Wearing love like the elegance that

Was her dress, her suit

Her gaze amused yet knowing that

Holy Spirit filled her up

And led her everyday

Friend loyal

Grandmother wise

Sassy businesswoman

It was an honor

to sit at her kitchen table

Or her beauty chair

Excited for a drop of

Feminine mystique

Or a tried and true recipe

A cool and classy mom

Swept away for a gentle sleep

She leaves us the sweet,

Unstoppable earthiness

That moves

Black motherhood

And sisterhood

Always…

Thank You...

Thank you Lord for life and planting your gifts inside me, "you never failed me yet." Thank you Jesus for your sacrifice and the example of how to walk, lead and follow. Thank you Holy Spirit for your comfort and guidance.

Thanks to my parents, George (R.I.P. Daddy-O) and Alberta Gillon for supporting me and honoring language and expression growing up in our home.

Thanks to my siblings, Sharon, Sidney and Jeffrey (R.I.P). Jeff you really loved words and I share this book in your honor. Thanks also to their children and my extended family for keeping it real.

Thanks to my gifted cousin, author and peach farmer Dori Sanders who is my literary shero. I'm listening!

I also want to thank author and Professor Thomas Sayers Ellis for challenging my writing.

I appreciate Dr. Yemi Akande for sharing my poetry with the world.

Thanks Professor and Historian Regennia Williams for lifting me up when I just didn't know! Long live Langston Hughes! Dr. Regina Nixon : "the prayers of the righteous availeth much".

Professor Jeffrey Brudney, and author/businessman Everett Pruitt: your consistent encouragement is appreciated!

Thanks Vince Robinson for keeping the mic open and available to the poetic community in Cleveland.

I extend my gratitude to Don Slocum and the Neighborhood Leadership Institute for being supportive and honoring my creativity.

It's been a long time coming after years of Open Mics in churches, birthday and house parties, lounges, concerts, funerals, Cleveland's office of the FBI (for real!) union halls, open places and spaces. I am blessed to have a network of friends and community activists who can learn and share from each other. Let us all hold on to the generosity of spirit and the hope of transformation. I love and appreciate you for putting up with my calls and disappearances so I can write and for showing up to all the readings and your posts on Facebook. Thanks Elise, Mary C, Simmie, Bob I., Robbie, Veronica B., Daria, and my late wonderful friend Ivory: In your own unique ways, you have blessed my poetic journey.

Recently the Lord sent some folks into my life that have truly motivated and inspired me to make real my dream of publishing poetry. To my Pastor, Richard Gibson and Elizabeth Baptist Church Family: It's good to be home! Thanks for the love, teaching and a warm place to serve.

Evangelist Deborah A. Wright, I appreciate your patience, faithfulness and how you bless others!

J.W., the best is yet to come…

To Contact Author:

Jacqueline E. Gillon

Email: jacquiewrites@gmail.com

Published by

Parablist Publishing House, Inc.

Email: parablistpublishing@yahoo.com

www.parablistbooksonline.com

www.ingramcontent.com/pod-product-compliance
Lightning Source LLC
Chambersburg PA
CBHW071750040426
42446CB00012B/2506